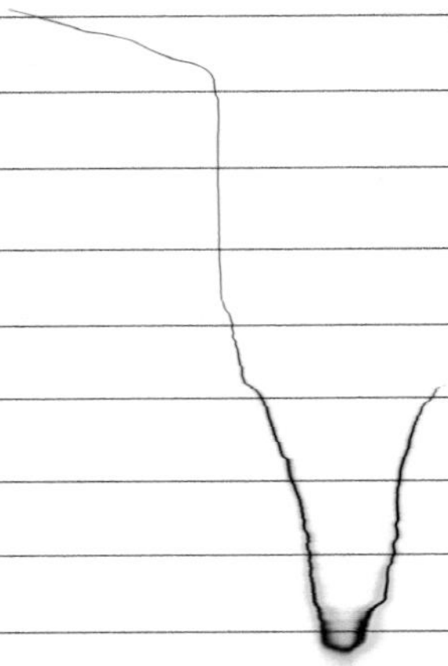

CPSIA information can be obtained
at www.ICGtesting.com
Printed in the USA
BVHW041341250420
578472BV00009B/2377

9 781097 449156